completing me

completing me

x.b. alloway

A life story through the eyes of a Pre-Teen to Teen

Palmetto Publishing Group
Charleston, SC

Completing Me
Copyright © 2018 by X.B. Alloway
All rights reserved

First Edition

Printed in the United States

ISBN-13: 978-1-64111-099-0
ISBN-10: 1-64111-099-6

This book is kept in it's original form from the time of inception to keep it pureness of voice for this age group.

To all who feel the need to be heard and no one has time to listen

To my family who is the epitome of love, especially my grandparents <3

X. B. Alloway

Today

Today will be like stepping-stones.

Don't let me fall and break my bones.

Or let me stay on the te-le-phone.

Through so many years I've grown!

I've earned this wonderful throne.

Who is the Perfect One?

Who is the Perfect One?

No one knows.

Who is the Perfect One?

Everyone wonders.

Who is the Perfect One?

Some people know.

Who the Perfect One is.

You Are the Most Amazing Person I Know

You are not like most people you listen to what I say.

You are the most amazing person I know.

When you smile you make me feel special.

You are the most amazing person I know.

When I'm in a bad mood you cheer me up.

You are the most amazing person I know.

When everyone else is mean to me you comfort me.

You are the most amazing person I know.

When I'm around you I glow like stars.

You are the most amazing person I know.

When you speak to me I feel as delicate as a rose.

You are the most amazing person I know.

Black Woman

We might be too much

Or you're just not enough

So just pass on by

While your train is still moving

Cause the black woman

Is not losing

You might be cute

You might be tall

But this black woman is standing strong

Devil

It might poison your food.

It might poison you brain.

But keep praying to God.

For it to go away.

It might be hard.

It might be rough.

But you just keep moving up.

Nightly Sounds

Cars blowing

What do they want?

Airplanes flying

Are they about to crash?

Heating unit

Are they cold or is it just clicking on?

Dogs barking

Is something wrong?

Cars on the highway

Where are they going?

Music from cars

Are they happy or sad?

What do you hear at night?

Blind in Love

You may think your blind in love.

That may be true.

But it's not your fault.

The man is playing games for you.

Waiting for you to come around.

But all he's making you do is fall to the ground.

Stand up to that man.

And let go of his hand.

All he is doing is fooling you.

With all his crazy moods.

Don't let him boss you around.

So you will end up having to be found.

Take control! Take charge!

Cause you should always be on guard.

The Most Amazing Boy

The most amazing boy is the sweetest boy I know.

The most amazing boy is the cutest

person I have ever seen.

The most amazing boy is the nicest person I know.

The most amazing acts as decent as a grown man.

The most amazing boy has a voice that suits him.

The most amazing boy is as loving as a puppy.

The most amazing boy to me is _____.

Wars

Wars are hurtful.

Wars are pain.

What's this world coming to?

Guilt and pain?

You may not see it coming.

But it's coming soon.

Don't let wars take you as a silly fool.

Some are weak.

Some are strong.

Don't let it sweep you right along.

Times are weary.

Drowned and deep.

It might come to you in your sleep.

My Love

My love is on the opposite side.

My love is not by my side.

My love is full of love then anger.

My love acts like he is not loveable.

My love's life is turned upside down.

My love is as good as it gets.

My love is a charming prince.

My love is an interesting scene.

My love is cute.

My love is fun.

My love is fine.

My love even makes me rhyme.

The Secret Man

Behind all the talk.

Behind all the boys.

There's something special.

For me to see.

He's been with me all summer long.

I'm just waiting for him to come along.

He's my inspiration every morning.

He keeps me laughing at every moment.

When I'm in pain he's my doctor.

When I'm stressed he's my counselor.

When he's gone that's all I think about.

When he smiles I feel great.

But will he ever come around?

I guess I'll find out soon.

But until then I love you and always will.

My Baby

My baby makes me feel shy.

My baby makes me feel fly.

My baby makes me smile.

My baby's always in style.

My baby always have girls around.

My baby's all around.

My baby is all about me.

The Chosen One

The chosen one is attracted by the frozen one.

He sees her as an idol.

He doesn't know that she almost worships him.

But she knows that he should worship her.

That's how it goes in the book of rules.

But who says the rules can't change.

Crazy Boys

Crazy boys always act crazy.

Crazy boys are crazy about girls.

Crazy boys try to show off.

Crazy boys are all of the best.

Crazy boys make you rhyme.

Crazy boys want to have fun.

Crazy boys want to hang.

Crazy boys want to bang.

Crazy boys, crazy boys, crazy boys.

Past Lust: Future Love

Right now it's lust.

You just need someone to hold.

Later it will be love.

Something to hold forever.

Lust or Love?

Which one is you?

Does it really matter?

Yes it does.

If you marry in the name of lust all you can

ask yourself is, where's the divorce papers?

If you marry in the name of love

It's everlasting

Together forever.

Love at First Sight

Love at first sight is when you see your love

then time stops.

Love at first sight is the most wonderful thing of life.

Love at first sight is not always the same.

Love at first sight you have no one to blame.

Love at first sight fills your heart with love.

Love at first sight is the best thing in the world.

Don't Break A Date

You might break a heart.

It will seem like your cruel.

Don't make excuses.

What if it happened to you?

Wouldn't you be mad?

Especially not happy.

You'll want to crawl in a hole.

With no one happy.

Think about others

Not just you

You'll never know how excited they may be

Then you'll never be forgiven for the second

time around.

Lazy

Some people choose to be lazy.

Some people choose to be crazy.

You can't blame it on sleep.

You can't blame it on how early you got up.

Being lazy is your fault.

If you want to do something

Don't be lazy and sleep.

Get up and do something

Basketball

It will be hard

Just stick it out

You'll want to quit

But people won't figure out

Why you want to quit the team

It's not as easy as it seems

You will shed some tears

But you'll make it through

Your coach will keep pushing you

To see what you can do

Put your trust in him

He'll see you through

He'll make you a better player

So you'll know what to do

If it's the sport you love

Why quit?

Dads

Sometimes they make you mad

Sometimes they make you glad

Sometimes they make you sad

Sometimes they make you proud

Sometimes they make you frown

Sometimes they make you smile

Dads turn your life upside down.

Cell Phones

You can talk.

You can text.

You can take pictures that are the best.

You're always on it.

It never leaves your side.

Busy

Always going around and around

It seems like time will never slow down

People riding all around

It's like a lunch rush upside down

You can never make time for things like family

Business always comes first

If you keep it up you'll end up in a slow riding hearse

Take a break here and there

Maybe you'll survive through these fine lines

Brothers

Brothers sometimes pick.

Sometimes they cry.

Sometimes they try to act fly.

Sometimes they get in trouble.

Sometimes they act nice.

Sometimes they are full of laughter.

Sometimes they are full of anger.

But no matter what you still have a brother.

Friends

How many friends do you have?

Maybe one or two or maybe a few.

All friends are not the same.

Some are mean. Some are shy.

Some are grumpy. Some are silly.

Some are crazy. Some are mad.

Some are sad. Some are nice.

Maybe you have all of these friends because

I know I do.

Heartbreaker

I know someone who is very cruel

I know he'll steal your favorite mule.

I know he'll say he love's you

But it's really not true.

He'll steal your heart so very fast

You won't believe it's true.

So watch out for that heartbreaker

Because he is very true.

True to you? Do you say?

Oh, yes he's very true.

So pack you bags very tight

Because he's coming for you too!

I Wish

I wish there was no hate.

I wish there were no grudges.

I wish people would keep their own opinion
to themselves.

I wish there always were fair people.

I wish there were always love.

I wish there was a very special place.

I wish someone were always proud.

I wish their hands would stay to themselves.

I wish there were easier decisions.

I wish people would think before they speak.

Think about what you would wish.

My Love: Part 2

My love is getting better

My love is coming to my side

My love is controlling his anger

My love is more charming than ever

My love is now loveable

My love's life is now right side up

My love is full of love

Wise Man

Why do you act so smart?

Do you know some other people can be right?

Let people explain before you speak.

When you explain make a short explanation,

Unless they ask for a long explanation.

So I hope you've learned a lesson.

Because you are not the wisest man.

Arguing With Like

I don't know if it's love yet.

Haven't known him long enough.

My mama doesn't like him.

But I really don't care.

Some things are missing.

But others filled in.

He deserves something good in his life.

It might not be me but,

It will do for now.

But he doesn't need her.

The person who breaks his heart.

She cheats on him like he's one hard test.

Who cheats back cause he doesn't feel he's her best.

It's over now and, he's moved on.

She won't let him go to someone,

Who wants him the most.

It's starting to piss her off.

The other girl doesn't care.

She'll get what she wants

No matter if anyone cares.

Spring

Rain tapping on my windowpane.

Butterflies are fluttering through the air.

Birds singing for a new day.

Bees buzzing happily for new flowers.

Grasshoppers hopping through green grasses.

Sun shining to make the flowers grow.

Bunnies hopping through the wondrous flowers.

Flowers blooming curiously.

People talking in the park.

Children playing excitedly.

Secret Relationship

A secret relationship is a hard thing to do.

You want to tell everyone.

But the other person will say it's untrue.

He'll blow you kisses that people can't see.

You'll be itching to yell that one little tree.

But you won't go with the story untold.

So you have to tell one little soul.

Songs

Some songs are good.

Some songs are great.

Some songs are meant to be late.

Some songs should have never been made.

Some songs are people's life.

Some songs to people are just songs.

Some songs are deep.

Some songs are shallow.

Some songs just make you want to stay sleepy hollow.

Some songs are crazy.

Some songs have influences.

Some songs you can halfway listen to.

Some songs you have to tune to every word.

A New Love

I found a new love.

One I can depend on.

One who will love me back.

One who will be by my side.

One who is wise.

One who is charming.

One who is my prince.

One who is handsome.

One who is popular.

One who is always going the right way.

This is my charming prince.

Cheating

If I cheated it was because I didn't love you.

Maybe it was love last year.

But this year is something more.

Something bigger and better for me to have.

He may have some problems but,

Their all solved.

We have a true love.

And you can't block it.

Our love is stronger than glue

Don't pull us apart.

Our love is like cement.

Always there til the end.

Smart Girls

Smart girls are mean.

Smart girls are nice.

Sometimes smart girls make you want to fight.

Sometimes smart girls have to pay the price.

Smart girls are popular.

Smart girls are jerks.

Sometimes smart girls make you want to smirk.

Smart girls are preppy.

Smart girls are flirts.

Sometimes smart girls like to wear skirts.

Smart girls are stupid.

Smart girls are fun.

Smart girls can make a lot of people feel dumb.

While I Was Cheating

While I was cheating.......

I wasn't thinking of you.

While I was cheating......

I was enjoying myself.

While I was cheating......

I was having fun.

While I was cheating......

I wasn't thinking of our future.

A New Life

To have a new life

You have to do things right

You have to pay some price

To have a new life

You have to think everything's all right

You have to stick to what you know.

Hopeless Romantic

Many people may thing they are hopeless romantic.

Going through divorce and kids.

You think the world around you is going to end.

But you'll be okay.

You'll make it through.

Everyone has that special someone that just

belongs to them.

You might have just got married too quick.

Or not gotten to know each other well enough.

Your first love is not always your true love.

So explore your options don't just settle for one.

Cause there are many fish in the sea.

Search for the big fish and let the little ones grow.

Look for the perfect one, the one your heart desires.

Don't fall short of your blessings cause

eventually they will come.

Be happy being single. Love you!

When you're happy and smiling a man

will find your radiant glow.

The Angry Man

The angry man is wishing for hope.

He's running out of time.

The clock's ticking fast.

I hope he hurries soon.

The sand's going through

Time is running fast

Too late

Time's up

Let's give an explanation to God

Why's the man so angry?

So, he lost his job.

Moments of Time

Moments of time

Passes by

Boring or fun

Things have to be done

Class work or homework

It's not fun

Time to clown

On these crazy Don Wons

In Love With a Bad Person

I never thought it would be

I thought it would have been if I couldn't see

In love with a bad person

Makes you feel like you're free

Until your mom breaks your knee

You'll fall like a tree

In love with a bad person

Now you can see

That the bad person you fell in love with isn't

for you and me

Feeling Like Giving Up

The person you've always loved no matter what

Tells you that he's through with you

You all have been through so much together

You have been by his side through thick and thin

We've practically made our vows and

One day later I hear "you're cut from my life'

Oh my gosh what am I to do

I feel so worthless

I have so much love for him

He just passed it up

His loss; someone's gain

I shed a few tears

But don't let him see a sweat

You will always love him but

Will never be with him

Don't go with him ever again

He broke your heart into tiny piece

He can't put them back together

But someone else can

Now he's wondering what he lost

From Love to Hope

Love is like a rose

A rose is like a dove

A dove is like freedom

Freedom is like hope

Hope is with you all the time

You will find it in a rhyme

Keep God First

Keep God first

No matter what you do

He will guide you through

He will mold you, and shape you

Into something new

A radiant glow coming from your soul

Everyone sees it and wonder could it be true

Could they have this life too?

Keep God first and anything's possible

Now think about John and Jacob too.

Think that's a mess, Noah sailed the flood blue

Missing You

With you not here it's like an endless road

With you here there's all hope to find an end

Missing you is like a burning meadow

When you are here the meadows are clear

When you are not here it's like dead meadows

When you're not around it's a gloomy world

When you're here I have a happy world

I look forward to seeing your loving face

I can't see you now

I'm just missing you

Sin to Obedience

Always drunk

Never free

The devil's going to get you

So fall on one knee

Bow to God

He can guard you

You'll be safe

Chris Brown

You were in the elevator with my mom

I know every word to every one of your songs

Saw you perform

Didn't get an autograph though

You left too quick

And I had a hissy fit

Always leaving at the nick of time

When are we going to get our time?

Mystery Love

Keeping close in wild dreams

My mystery love needs to be seen

Lonely as it seems

I need to be strong

To find this sad song

A song waiting to be sung

When this song is sung by the right one

There will be an amazing tune

It will stick in your brain til it finds a tune

Saw an Old Love

I saw an old love

He wouldn't speak to me

He was just quietly followed

Oops, dropped my papers

Didn't offer to get them

Just sat and stared

Maybe in a bad mood

If I had seen him sooner

Would it be more exciting?

The question still follows

Does he really love me?

Reunion

Saw a very old friend

He seemed glad to see me

He looked like an over grown tree

His hair was so bushy

His eyes are so brown

It seems like he never could have been found

School

Going to school can make you feel cool

So you won't feel like a fool

And have to work with old tools

Making raggedy old stools

So you should choose the right school

So you won't feel like a fool

Gossip

Gossip is fake.

Gossip is not great.

It makes people sad.

Then people get mad.

Then you will be sad.

Because they are hunting you down.

You have permanent frowns.

No crowns.

If you think gossip is great,

Then you need some help

You need to yelp, yelp, yelp.

Back in Business

I talked to my old love again.

He is nicer than ever.

But, I will stick with just friends.

I wouldn't want to ruin it again.

Away on Business

Away on business seems like everyday.

The more and more you have to pray.

That your parents will come back one day.

Maybe they'll get to stay.

Then you'll fly away

And be happy everyday.

Hard Work

Hard work takes dedication

Hard work takes time

Hard work should always be on minds

Big and tall, little or small

Hard work follows you all of the time

To Young

To young to do this or that

All we have is knick-knacks

Too young? Maybe you're too old.

Let us enjoy life being young

Before we become too old

Pretty Slave

Pretty slave speak up

Pretty slave open up

Who will ever hear our cry?

Not the master, nor the cook

We will walk by foot

Shout it loud

Strong and proud

Pretty slave speak up

Dear Piano

Dear piano you are so soft

Piano you're so true

Your sound makes me turn blue

Not the way it sounds

It's the perfect mood

Your keys are so slick

Your chords are so cool

Dear piano it's all on you

Missing My Brother

I'm missing my brother with nothing to do

I miss him so much I look for his shoe

But, I'm not the only one missing this dude

He could be a star on Family Feud

He could sing his favorite tune

Without doing something and having to be sued

Missing my brother that's so new

But, I hope he misses me too

Someone Special

Someone special could be anybody

Big, tall, little, or small

My someone special

Is dark and handsome

I love him like I love myself

He's much more than just a man

He's someone special in my hands

A Love for Someone New

A love for someone new

This just can't be true

Need to clear my head

Something has to be said

I love him so much

But there's someone new

He's stuck on you

Don't hold him so tight

With all of your might

Maybe I have a chance

With this lovely man

What's going wrong

With this lovely song

I want him so bad

It's making me sad

Love

The way your soul

Blends into my heart

Makes me crave

You're so brave

Your eyes are so deep

Just like a sea

I'm floating on shore

Don't let me drown

I miss you every second

You're apart of my world

Your hair is so sexy

But not as sexy as you

I love you with all my heart

Deep inside I know you love me too

I'm blessed to know a man like you

You're so smart

I love that in a man

You're special to me

I hope I'm special to you

Get Well Soon

Get well soon

So you can have the moon

And be in a good mood

Just like a raccoon

All day until noon

So please please get well soon

A Love No More

He was the love of my life

Talking to someone else

In my face he'd be so true

But underneath he's all so blue

I deserve more than him

More than he could ever be

Someone who call me by my true name

Bree

Someone Who Tells
Lies About You

You want to know who it is

So, you can give them a piece of your mind

You might want to break their bones

But that's too violent for sure

You probably see them everyday

They watch your every move

You turn and walk away

But they will just follow you

So, they can start another rumor

To ruin your holiday cheer

I bet they wouldn't say that stuff

If you were very near

How Basketball Makes You Feel

It makes you feel popular

It makes you feel free

When you fall you hope you don't break your knee

You score a basket

The points add up

The buzzer sneaks up

BUZZ!!!

You win the game!

High School

You come to it to learn

You come to it to study

You come to it to socialize

You must always focus your eyes

On all of the messy people

That walk to and fro

The boys that make fun of you

Through and through

The teachers who see everything

Or the ones that don't see enough

The subs who are through the roof

Through some are through the ground

High school oh high school

Will turn you upside down

Always on Punishment

With all that attitude

All that mouth

Your mama doesn't like it

Cause she sees her in you

The only reason you're on punishment

Is cause she doesn't want you to be like her

With two kids

And a step dad

But it's ok

You'll make it through

Being a better person

Than YOU thought

Happy Birthday

Happy times

Your favorite day

All good luck

Wishes coming true

Parties all through

Laughter filling the air

Guys all in your hair

Your family's happy

All for you

Friends lift you up

To keep your spirits high

Make the most of this day

Cause it's gonna fly by

From Nothing to Everything

He used to think nothing of me

He thought I was just some girl

He got to know me better

We got closer in friendship

Discussing everything in his life

From friendships to relationships

I put up with torture and abuse

But only for a short while

He's starting to realize I'm something more

He invited me to the movies

I've talked to his mama

He's starting to show interest

Showering me with kisses

Being nice too me and having a good time

I wonder how far this will go

It's hard to transform a guy into what you want

But I did it

It's been accomplished

But how will my family reply?

Someone Who Has Changed

You've changed from this to that

I don't know if it's real

I don't want to give you my heart

Cause you're such a jokester

I don't know when you're serious

I hope you are

Because my feelings go deep for you

I try to keep them stored away in a tiny box

I don't want to show weakness

I know that's how you feel

Don't want to show weakness

Around all your friends who think you're the boss

Did you know you can be sensitive and tough?

You don't have to prove anything to anyone

Picking on other people doesn't get you gratification

Being nice could get you gratification too

I Think I Love You

I think I love you

But I'm afraid to give you my heart

You might break it

If you do I don't think I could take it

Sometimes I think I can read your signs

But when you flip the script

And act totally different

I don't know what to do with myself

I like the new you

But I don't know if it's the true you

I want to know

If it's the true you then I want to be with you

But I won't ask you out this time

It has to be you

That's how I will know if it's true

If I say yes, then I'll also say

"I do."

Like A Christmas Tree

Love is like a Christmas tree

Sometimes it lights up

Sometimes it blinks

Like when your heart is happy

And it starts to fade away

Sometimes it's colorful

Sometimes it's just one color

It's like being bubbly or

Just being happy, mad, or glad

Goshen Seniors of 2007

I'll miss all the laughs

All the joys you bring

The daily arguments

The clowning from time to time

The smiles for days

The pranks that are never to be beaten

The grades for the greatest parent

The outfits that make a fashion show worthwhile

The love that fills the room when one walks in

The spirit of a team captain

I love the seniors of '07!

They never bring pain!

Someone Who Likes You
but Won't Tell You

He has a girlfriend

It would be ok

If it wasn't my enemy

She stares him down

All times of the day

She stares other girls too

Cause she's so confused

I've had him before

It was a relationship so good

He still wants me but

I'm so misunderstood

I want him too

But he will be gone soon

Trying to make the best of it I can

There's only four months left

Time is slipping away

I hope he opens up

Before it passes away

Watching Me in All the Right Ways

You have me by a thread

Twirled around your finger

Could have me by your side

Looking amongst a standing figure

But yet you're with that other chick

We know we need each other

So why are you trying to front?

We will have miserable lives

Until we meet again

We love each other nothings going to change

That's 'til the end

I Love You!

I love you

Why can't you accept it to be true?

I miss every second of you

And that's a long time too

We talk about being together

But it won't come true

I mean yes it will

But not right now

You're almost in college

I'm in high school

What's going to happen to me?

While you're out there being a fool

Don't come back and try to say you love me

If you loved me you would have told me sooner!

You need to tell me now

Before you get too proud

Tell me tonight

When I'm in bed and on the prowl

Single for Too Long

I've been single for too long

I'm starting to feel the loneliness

I don't like not having someone to call baby

Somcone to cuddle with in the day

And talk to at night

The only thing that keeps me company are my

bears and paper

Everyone has someone except for me

I hate being lonely

Hate being alone

But in patience brings greatness

Mirror

Have you ever heard of making love in a mirror?

Sounds interesting huh?

Try it one day

Tell me if you like it

Let me know its aspects

I love hearing about love

Love is an important thing

So, put some excitement in your life and

make love in front of a mirror

Months

January- the month of resolutions no one
will follow them
February- this month is filled up with
many important birthdays including the
fact that it's black history month
March- the cold is starting to ease off
and everyone's cheering up
April- the month of my birthday
always a special month
May- the month schools out;
nothing but fun all the way

June- a very special friend's birthday;

nothing more special than a friend

July- my mom's month, it belongs to

only her and my grandma

August- school starts back. YIPPEE!!!!

September- the leaves start falling for us to pick up

October- time for Halloween TRICK OR TREAT!

November- time to give thanks

December- the month of which my savior

was born; my Lord's son to watch over us

But all year-round love is in its place. EVERYWHERE!

Someone Who Tries to Make You Mad on Purpose

I don't think it's intentional

But it seems to be true

She flipping her hair around

Cause she thinks I'm watching you

But she's your cousin

She wants to be more

She flirts with him 24/7

Like I'm some kind of whore

I'm good for you

It's just so true

But she's cheating on her man

Like he's gonna stand

For what's going down

It's been all around town

Everybody knows

He will too

Soon or later they will break up

Cause she's playing as such a fool

Someone Who Ignores You

He's had special times with you

Then he has someone new

It's like you don't exist

But doesn't even like her

He wants you

He has a funny way of showing it

He looks at you with disgust

You see him with tears in your eyes

Cause there's so much fire

Acting Funny

Someone's acting funny

Playing with my head

He knows I like him

But I guess he doesn't really care

He flirts with other girls

My friends try to cheer me up

But I can't keep from staying down

Wanting to Cry

I'm wanting to cry

Every second of the day

Just break down in tears

For years and years

Love can break your heart

And give it away

Away to the dumpster

He will break it into tiny pieces

And think nothing else about it

Walking in circles around you

Talking about other people

Wasting My Time

I'm wasting my time

Thinking about this boy

If he hasn't told me he likes me yet

I guess that I can make my best

Of something new

Someone who I know can choose

In Love With Somebody
and Nobody Knows It

The only person who knows it is me and that person

We get so excited to see each other

Cause everything is so perfect

We write letters to express our feelings

But there are so many in just dealings

The days pass but still no one knows

He gets suspended I get sent a rose

But nothing changes everything remains the same

In love with somebody and nobody

knows it is so insane

Found Out You're My Cousins

Today I found out two people were my cousins

The people I wanted to talk to

Are now my cousins?

I can't believe it

It can't be true

After all this stuff that I done been through

So, take my advice

And seek in another state

Because this might make you wide awake

The person you are dating could be your cousin

So, check out the history all above you

In Love With Somebody
You Don't Need

He does mean things to you

And you just let it go

He's taking advantage of you

And it's so true

But you love him

You really do

Then again he talks to girls under

All he is doing is boosting your head

And your one true love won't do that to you

So, let him go

And move on

Cause he's not the one for you

In Love With Somebody
Who Won't Be Approved

They love me so much

But it probably wouldn't ever be

Anything too serious

Like you asking to marry me

My family would say no

But I would say yes

You have shown me so much love

More than all these other boys could

So, don't give up hope

Help is coming soon

Don't worry baby

But be patient

We'll make it through

So Much to Say

I have so much to say

It has to stay quiet

Cause some feelings may be hurt

Some hearts may be lifted

But mine will be satisfied

Have a lot to get off of my chest

But I'm a do my best

Keep it simple

Don't try and confuse

People getting too slow these days

Have to pray for them

So, I will be happy

When I have said what I got to say

Someone Who thinks Everything's My Fault

Take some of the blame

It's mutual fault

He does some things

I do some too

Everyone asks, "Why did ya'll break up?"

I reply. "I don't know. Ask him."

He has no reply

So, this relationship must die

Sometimes he tries to spit game

Other times he's acting like fame

I don't like it

He must don't want me back

He doesn't try hard enough

I told him how I feel

I have nothing else to say

So, do what you got to do

Cause I'ma get mine

Just remember I will always love you!

You Wanting Me Back

You want me back

And I still love you

You made me wait all this time

I want you back

I know it won't be the same

But I love you

A Clean Slate

I broke up with my boyfriend

A clean slate again

He broke a little of my heart

But I think I'll still live

I still have love for him

He still can be mine

I don't know if we were made for the end of time

But I know we were made to do the right thing

I just don't know when

In Love with You and Not Cause of Looks

I'm in love with you and it's not for looks

Your personality is great.

No matter what anyone says

You love me for who I am

Not for what I look like

We connect souls every time we meet

When we hug it feels as though we turn into one

You are my other half

My heart

My soul

You cherish me with all good things

I thank you from the bottom of my heart

You are the most honest person I know

I love that about you

I appreciate everything that you do

And I love you for it

A Mother

A mother will put you through so many things

Hurt. Pain. Sorrow. Or disdain

But no matter how much you go through

There will be one person to support you

It will be your mother to cheer you on

To reach your goal in life

She wants to see you succeed

So, make her proud

And work for her

When the Pain Comes

When the pain comes

Don't shy away

Face that pain right in the face

And knock it far away

Don't let people bring you pain

Kick them out of your life

If You Love Something
or Someone

If you love something.........

Don't stop reaching for it!

If you love someone..........

Don't let them get away!

If you love something.........

Go and get it!

If you love some one...........

See if they love you back!

If you love something..........

Try your hardest to get it!

If you love someone............

Don't just do it for looks!

If you love something.........

Make sure it's worth something!

If you love someone.............

Love them to the fullest!

Candles

Candles set the mood

Candles calm your nerves

Candles make a room smell good

Candles provide light

Candles provide fire

Candles can make a room feel private

Letting Go of Baggage

Past relationships add on baggage

In my life I have plenty

I have one whose a past long term love

I have another past long-term love

They are stacked on top of each

other like 1,000 full suitcases

One is way heavier than the others

You should shed baggage before

entering another relationship

Acting Like You Hate Me

I could care less about you hating me

Because I know who loves me

I know God loves me because it was meant to be

I know my friends love me cause they

are as loyal as they can be

I know my family loves me cause they

do more than I could ever see

But why would I care if you love me

I love you so what

But the only reason I love you is cause

your mama didn't do it enough

About the Author

X. B. Alloway has a bachelor's degree from Troy University in political science with a concentration in international politics and a minor in philosophy, and as of December 2017 completed her master's degree through their online program. She began writing in poetry at the age of nine and was influenced by growing up in Georgia and Alabama, where she was accepted to the Alabama School of Math and Science. This is her first of three forthcoming books of poetry.

Made in the USA
Columbia, SC
02 July 2024

37961649R00067